FUNNIES OF THE PRESIDENTS

From Mount Rushmore To Laugh More:
Presidential Gags, Gaffes, Goofs,
and Gut-Busters

ChatGPT
and
Paul Lloyd Hemphill

DEDICATION

To teenagers facing the challenges of leadership and life:
may you find inspiration in these stories of laughter from
our nation's presidents. Remember, even the most serious
leaders had their funny moments, proving that humor can
lighten the load. Embrace your own journey with a smile,
and never underestimate the power of a good laugh to
help you through tough times.

This non-fiction book is available for educational, business, or promotional use. Who knew learning could be this fun? For more information, contact the author directly at paul@inspirationforteens.com

FUNNIES OF THE PRESIDENTS

Library of Congress Control Number: 2024921936
Paperback ISBN: 978-1-7377416-8-8

1. Political Humor 2. Biography 3. U.S. History 4. Non-Fiction

Introduction

This book is a journey through the laughter and lighthearted moments that have dotted the often serious landscape of America's past.

While our presidents have had their share of successes and failures—some truly great and others, well, let's say they didn't quite hit the mark—this collection isn't about politics. Instead, it focuses on the funny stories that remind us these leaders were, above all, human.

Take James Monroe, for example, who turned a White House dinner into a full-blown food riot - chicken flew, plates smashed, and guests were left wondering if they'd accidentally wandered into a cafeteria brawl!

Then there's Andrew Jackson, whose pet parrot could have outdone any comedian with its knack for yelling curse words at unsuspecting guests. Imagine trying to enjoy a dignified dinner while being serenaded by a bird with a mouth like a sailor!

Don't forget Abraham Lincoln, whose storytelling ability was so sharp that he could make even the grimmest faces crack a smile. And let's not skip over JFK's dad jokes, which were so corny they'd make even a popcorn kernel roll its eyes.

From quirky anecdotes to hilarious mishaps, we dive into the lighter side of each president's time in office. You'll discover how they handled awkward situations, cracked jokes, and sometimes stumbled in the most amusing ways. In a world filled with heavy news, it's important to remember that laughter Is a powerful force that connects us all.

So, whether you're a history buff or just looking for a good laugh, *Funnies of the Presidents* invites you to see the fun behind the facade of our nation's leaders. Get ready to chuckle, snicker, and giggle as we explore the amusing tales that have shaped the stories of those who've held the highest office in the land!

Paul Lloyd Hemphill
(ChapGPT took a well-earned time off for 5 seconds!)

TABLE OF CONTENTS

George Washington
1789-1797

George Washington, our first president and a meticulous leader, wasn't immune to moments of awkwardness. Known for his attention to detail, especially regarding his appearance, Washington prided himself on maintaining a dignified presence during the Revolutionary War; however, one day, his usual composed image took a humorous turn.

Preparing for an important meeting, Washington discovered that his favorite pair of custom-made pants had mysteriously vanished. His staff searched frantically but couldn't locate them. With time running out, Washington had no choice but to wear an old, ill-fitting pair of trousers that barely reached his ankles.

Determined to maintain his dignity, Washington entered the meeting, hoping no one would notice his awkward attire. But, it wasn't long before people observed their normally well-dressed commander looking as though he were bracing for a flood. His too-short pants left his socks exposed, drawing curious glances from all around.

Throughout the meeting, Washington remained serious and focused, despite the subtle smiles and sideways glances from his officers. Though no one dared to laugh out loud—after all, who would risk offending the general—the struggle to suppress a grin was palpable.

Washington, ever composed, took the situation in stride, carrying on with his duties despite the wardrobe malfunction. After the meeting, his favorite pants were eventually found, neatly folded under his bed where he had left them.

This light-hearted episode reveals a relatable, human side of George Washington. Even in his role as commander of the Continental Army, he experienced the same everyday mishaps we all do—a reminder that even history's greatest figures had their moments of unintentional comedy.

John Adams
1797-1801

John Adams, the second president of the United States, was known for his unwavering dedication to the country and his fiery temper. But he also had moments of humor that make him more relatable, especially his rather absurd horseback-ride to his own inauguration in 1797.

As Adams prepared for the long journey to Philadelphia to assume the presidency, most dignitaries would have traveled in a stately carriage. But not Adams. He opted to make the trip on horseback. Nothing quite says "I'm about to lead the nation" like arriving on a sweaty, uncomfortable horse ride.

The journey was far from smooth. Adams, not exactly a slim figure and well into his sixties, bounced uncomfortably in the saddle for miles. According to accounts, it was a rough ride, and he grumbled the entire way, like an old man forced into a high school reunion he had no interest in attending.

When he finally reached Philadelphia, Adams was sore, dusty, and undoubtedly regretting his choice. Rather than making a dignified entrance, he looked more like a disheveled cowboy who had lost his way. Sweaty and exhausted, with the look of a man in desperate need of a nap, Adams greeted the citizens. They must have been thrilled but also slightly puzzled that this was their new president.

Adding to the humor, Adams had the daunting task of following George Washington, who was known for his majestic, almost regal demeanor. Adams himself once referred to his role as Washington's "poor successor," and his awkward entrance only emphasized that contrast.

Despite the less-than-grand entrance, Adams' dedication to toughing it out on horseback became a legendary part of his quirky personality. It serves as a reminder that even America's early presidents had their share of unintentional, hilarious moments.

Thomas Jefferson
1801-1809

Thomas Jefferson, a founding father and the third president of the United States, was not only an intellectual giant but also had his share of humorous moments. One particularly amusing episode occurred during his tenure as ambassador to France in the late 1780s, involving a prank, an unusual animal, and a lot of confused French onlookers.

While in Paris, Jefferson became fascinated by a unique North American creature—the moose. At that time, he was embroiled in a debate with European scientists, particularly the French naturalist Count Buffon, who had claimed that North American animals were inferior in size and strength. Jefferson took this assertion personally and sought to prove Buffon wrong in a decidedly extravagant way: by shipping a full-sized moose to Paris.

Yes, you read that correctly. Jefferson arranged for a massive, dead moose to be packed up and sent across the Atlantic. He even had it stuffed to present it as a trophy. Picture the bewilderment of the French aristocracy when this oversized, peculiar animal arrived in Paris, exuding the unmistakable scent of taxidermy and confusion.

Jefferson displayed the moose to Buffon and other European scholars, essentially declaring, "See! North American animals are just as grand as yours!" While there's no conclusive evidence that Buffon was fully convinced, Jefferson certainly felt triumphant. His quirky mission to defend the honor of American wildlife—and America itself—had been accomplished in one of the most unusual and amusing ways imaginable.

Imagine being one of Jefferson's aides, responsible for preparing this dead moose for its international journey. "Can you ensure the moose is packed securely? It has a boat to catch." Then explaining to French customs officials why a giant stuffed moose was arriving. This episode remains one of the most entertaining examples of presidential antics in the name of American pride.

James Madison
James Madison
1809-1817

James Madison, the fourth president of the United States and the principal architect of the Constitution, is often seen as a serious and intellectual figure. However, even Madison had his lighthearted moments, including one that nearly sparked a fashion revolution during his presidency.

Standing at just 5'4" and weighing around 100 pounds, Madison earned the nickname "Little Jemmy." Despite his small stature, he was married to the lively and stylish Dolley Madison, who was the life of every party and defined the role of First Lady. Dolley was renowned for her extravagant outfits, glamorous social events, and effortless charm, while James preferred to keep things simple and reserved—especially when it came to fashion.

During Madison's time in office, men's fashion favored tight, knee-length breeches. Madison, however, disliked these uncomfortable garments and instead opted for looser trousers. This unconventional choice caused a stir during a formal event when the president arrived wearing his beloved trousers, shocking Washington's elite. The sight of the president rejecting the fashionable breeches in favor of something so unstylish made quite the impression.

Yet, in a humorous twist, Madison's laid-back fashion statement inadvertently set a new trend. Men began abandoning their tight breeches for the comfort of looser trousers, all thanks to the president's refusal to conform to uncomfortable fashion standards. It was as if today's president attended a state dinner in sneakers, and soon everyone ditched their dress shoes.

While Dolley likely had to manage the fallout, giving Madison a playful eye-roll, James had the last laugh. He unintentionally became a fashion icon—not for his style, but for making comfort acceptable. Even presidents, it seems, understand the eternal dilemma of fashion versus comfort, and Madison unapologetically chose comfort!

James Monroe
1817-1825

James Monroe, the fifth president of the United States, is often remembered for serious achievements like the Monroe Doctrine; however, he also had a more lighthearted moment during his presidency, particularly with one memorable—and disastrous—White House party.

In 1820, Monroe decided to host a large public reception at the White House to celebrate the Fourth of July. His idea was simple: bring together citizens from all walks of life to boost national pride in a patriotic setting. What could go wrong?

Unfortunately, Monroe didn't anticipate the sheer excitement of the American people. Word spread that the president was offering free food and drinks to anyone who wanted to attend. Soon enough, thousands of eager guests flocked to the White House, transforming it into something resembling a massive block party.

The dignified event quickly spiraled into chaos. People pushed their way inside, devouring the food and, naturally, indulging in copious amounts of alcohol. Guests grabbed food with their hands, stuffed bread into their pockets, and drank like it was the last party on Earth. What began as a formal reception became a food frenzy.

As the crowd grew uncontrollable, Monroe's staff had to open windows and pass food out to people who couldn't fit inside. The White House had turned into a rowdy tailgate party. To make matters worse, even after the party was officially over, guests lingered, treating the White House like their personal hangout. Some even broke furniture, leaving behind a monumental mess that took days to clean up.

Monroe's attempt to connect with the public resulted in one of the wildest parties in White House history. After that, it's safe to assume Monroe thought twice about inviting the entire nation over for a party again!

J. Q. Adams

John Quincy Adams
1825-1829

John Quincy Adams, the sixth president of the United States, was known for his intellect and seriousness, but he also had some truly unusual habits. One of the most bizarre—and amusing—stories about him involves his early morning swims and a persistent journalist who snagged an interview in an unforgettable way.

Adams had a unique daily routine: he would swim naked in the Potomac River every morning at 5 a.m. That's right—before starting his day as president, Adams would strip down and take a nude dip in the river. It was his version of staying fit, long before the days of gym memberships or morning jogs.

Enter Anne Royall, one of America's first female journalists. Royall had been seeking an interview with Adams for some time, but he continually declined her requests. Frustrated but resourceful, Royall devised a clever and bold plan. Knowing about Adams' swimming routine, she made her way to the Potomac one morning while he was enjoying his daily dip.

As Adams emerged from the water, Royall appeared and grabbed his clothes, holding them hostage. With no way to dress and in a very vulnerable situation, Adams was forced to negotiate. Royall refused to return his clothes unless he agreed to an interview. Left with no alternative, Adams reluctantly gave in to her demands.

Thus, Royall became one of the first women to interview a sitting president, while Adams was left with one of the strangest presidential anecdotes in history.

Though Adams is remembered for his political acumen and dedication to public service, this humorous incident proves that even the most serious figures can find themselves in awkward situations—like being ambushed during a skinny-dip by a determined journalist.

Andrew Jackson
1829-1837

Andrew Jackson, the seventh president of the United States, was famous for his tough, no-nonsense demeanor, but one of the funniest and most unexpected stories about him involves a surprising antagonist: his pet parrot, Poll.

Yes, Jackson, known for his rough military background and fiery temper, had a pet parrot. Poll, gifted to him, was a smart bird with a knack for mimicking the language it heard. Given Jackson's reputation for colorful language, it's no surprise that the parrot picked up a few choice words over time.

Poll became a beloved, if somewhat foul-mouthed, fixture in the Jackson household. While Jackson was alive, Poll's habit of cursing might have been amusing, but things took a hilarious and bizarre turn after Jackson's death in 1845.

At Jackson's funeral, a solemn and dignified service was planned to honor the life of the strong-willed president. Friends, family, and political figures gathered to pay their respects. However, Poll the parrot had other ideas. In the midst of the service, Poll began squawking—loudly and profanely. The bird unleashed a stream of curse words that Jackson himself might have been proud of.

The guests were shocked, unsure whether to laugh or cry as Poll's swearing escalated. According to some accounts, the parrot's language became so inappropriate that it had to be removed from the funeral entirely.

This strange, yet hilarious, incident is a perfect reflection of the unpredictable nature of Jackson's life. Even in death, Jackson couldn't escape a bit of controversy—this time, courtesy of his foul-mouthed parrot.

While Jackson is remembered for his political and military achievements, he also holds the distinction of being the only U.S. president whose funeral was hilariously interrupted by a cursing parrot.

Martin Van Buren
1837-1841

Martin Van Buren, the eighth president of the United States, had a number of political achievements, but he also had a hilariously bizarre moment involving an attempt to fix his public image—one that backfired spectacularly.

After serving as president from 1837 to 1841, Van Buren wasn't particularly popular. His political opponents often mocked him, especially for his aristocratic demeanor and polished appearance. Always immaculately dressed, Van Buren tried to project a refined image, but this wasn't what stuck with the public.

Van Buren's nickname, "Old Kinderhook," stemmed from his birthplace in Kinderhook, New York. During his 1840 re-election campaign, his supporters tried to turn the nickname into a rallying cry. They began using "O.K." as an abbreviation for "Old Kinderhook," hoping it would make him seem more relatable and down-to-earth, like he was "okay" with the people.

But the strategy completely backfired. Instead of making Van Buren appear approachable, his critics seized on "O.K." and started using it sarcastically. Rather than associating "O.K." with Van Buren in a positive light, people began using it dismissively, as in, "Oh, that's just O.K.," to mock his campaign's attempt to make him seem cool and relatable.

Ironically, while Van Buren's political career didn't benefit from this slogan, the phrase "O.K." took on a life of its own. It became ingrained in American slang, and eventually spread around the world as a common way to express approval or acknowledgment.

So, the next time you say "O.K.," remember that it originated as a failed rebranding effort by Van Buren's supporters. Though he didn't win re-election, Van Buren inadvertently gave us one of the most enduring phrases in modern language!

William Henry Harrison
1841

William Henry Harrison's presidency is best remembered for his infamous inauguration day, which led to the shortest term in U.S. history—all because he refused to wear a coat.

Picture this: It's March 4, 1841, and Harrison, 68 years old, has just been elected the ninth president of the United States. Determined to prove he's as tough as ever, Harrison is ready to show off his vigor. The problem? The weather in Washington, D.C., is awful—cold, windy, and pouring rain. Most people would have bundled up, but not Harrison.

In a display of stubborn toughness, Harrison steps out to give his inaugural address without a coat, hat, or gloves, as if to prove his resilience. While the crowd shivers in the miserable weather, Harrison stands proudly in just his suit, braving the elements.

To make matters worse, he delivers the longest inaugural speech in American history. At nearly two hours and over 8,000 words, Harrison rambles about policy, philosophy, and everything in between while everyone, including himself, continues to freeze in the rain.

The result of this bravado? A severe cold that quickly turned into pneumonia. Harrison, still determined to tough it out, ignored his worsening symptoms. Just 31 days after taking office, on April 4, 1841, Harrison died, making his presidency the shortest in U.S. history.

Rather than earning respect for his toughness, Harrison became a historical cautionary tale. His refusal to dress appropriately for the weather, combined with his marathon speech, ultimately cost him his life—and his legacy. He is remembered not for his policies, but as the president who couldn't survive his own inauguration.

The lesson from Harrison's misstep? Sometimes, it's better to wear a coat and keep the speech short—especially when your presidency is on the line.

John Tyler
1841-1845

John Tyler, the tenth president of the United States, is remembered for an unusual and amusing chapter in White House history, largely thanks to his large family and their mischievous antics involving goats.

Tyler, the first vice president to assume the presidency after the death of William Henry Harrison, made history in the process. But his personal life captured just as much attention. With 15 children from two marriages, Tyler holds the record for the most kids of any U.S. president. His White House often felt more like a lively family home than a government office.

Tyler's younger children, especially his sons, were known for their high energy and creative play. Among their favorite pastimes? Goat races. While other presidents had traditional pets like dogs or birds, Tyler's children had a pair of goats that they harnessed to small carts. The kids raced up and down the White House halls, treating the residence like their own private rodeo. Visitors to the White House would sometimes find their serious discussions interrupted by racing goats and shouting children.

The chaos didn't stop indoors. One day, the children took their goat races outside onto the White House lawn, creating even more mayhem. The goats reportedly knocked over furniture and caused disorder, turning the grounds into a playful chaos. These races became a regular occurrence, leaving dignitaries and visitors alike bewildered by the president's free-spirited household.

Tyler, likely absorbed by the political challenges of his presidency, seemed to overlook his children's antics. As a result, his White House became famous for its goat-powered races, creating a humorous legacy that outlasted his political achievements. While Tyler's presidential record may be less remembered, his children's wild goat races left a lasting mark on American history.

James K. Polk
1845-1849

James K. Polk, the 11th president of the United States, is best known for being a workaholic and overseeing territorial expansion during the Mexican-American War. However, one of the funniest and most bizarre aspects of his presidency was his grumpy, no-nonsense attitude, which made him more infamous for being humorless than for any single event.

Polk's all-business demeanor led to an unintentionally comical moment that highlighted just how little time he had for anything fun—particularly when it came to something as simple as music. After taking office in 1845, Polk quickly established himself as one of the most serious men ever to occupy the White House. He worked long hours, rose early, and filled his schedule to the brim, much to the exhaustion of his staff. Anything he deemed unnecessary or unproductive was strictly forbidden, including activities most people consider enjoyable—like dancing.

Polk, along with his equally no-nonsense wife, Sarah, banned dancing and card games at all White House functions. While other first ladies hosted grand balls and lively parties, the Polks transformed the White House into a somber place where fun was off-limits. The atmosphere became so dull that guests frequently joked about how stiff and boring the Polks' events were.

The most amusing story came during a state dinner when a guest, hoping to liven things up, suggested playing some music. Most presidents would agree that music could improve the ambiance, but not Polk. Instead, he reportedly gave the guest a stern look and shut down the idea, leaving everyone in awkward silence.

Polk's humorless reputation became a running joke, and he earned the title of "the least fun president." While Polk accomplished much during his presidency, including the annexation of Texas and the Oregon Territory, he is also remembered as the man who banned fun—grumbling even about music as a waste of time.

Zachary Taylor
1849-1850

Zachary Taylor, the 12th president of the United States, was a rugged war hero, not a polished politician, and his rough-around-the-edges approach became evident the moment he stepped into the White House. Having spent over 40 years in the U.S. Army, leading troops rather than crafting speeches, Taylor treated the presidency like just another military assignment —with a lot more paperwork.

One of the most amusing moments of his presidency, and clear proof that Taylor didn't quite grasp the political theater of the role, came during his own inauguration. By 1849, presidential inaugurations were grand affairs, filled with speeches and fanfare. The expectation was simple: the new president would deliver an inspiring address, full of lofty promises. But Taylor wasn't interested in playing along.

He famously skipped his own inauguration rehearsal, likely thinking, "I've commanded troops in battle—how hard can it be to deliver a speech?" Turns out, it was harder than he expected. When his big day arrived on March 4, 1849, Taylor refused to give the lengthy, traditional speech everyone anticipated. Instead, he stood at the podium, said a few brief lines, and called it a day, leaving the crowd confused and wondering, "That's it? That's our new president?"

The confusion didn't end there. Since his inauguration fell on a Sunday, Taylor refused to take the oath of office, believing it improper to do so on the Sabbath. As a result, the United States technically had no president for 24 hours until Taylor was sworn in on Monday, March 5. For a day, the country was left in an awkward limbo.

Taylor's unorthodox approach made one thing clear—he wasn't going to be a typical president. His laid-back, unconventional style set the tone for a presidency remembered more for its quirky moments than any grand legacy.

Millard Fillmore
1850-1853

Millard Fillmore, the 13th president of the United States, is one of those historical figures that tends to be forgotten. He wasn't known for bold decisions or memorable speeches, but rather, for something hilariously absurd: a completely made-up story about how he installed the first bathtub in the White House.

In 1917, decades after Fillmore had left office, journalist H.L. Mencken, known for his sharp wit and sarcasm, decided to play a prank on history. He wrote a fake article claiming that Fillmore had heroically installed the first bathtub in the White House. But Mencken didn't stop there—he embellished the tale with absurd details about Fillmore's obsession with cleanliness and how the nation had been in a hygiene crisis until Fillmore came to the rescue with his glorious porcelain tub.

The twist? Everyone believed it. What was intended as a joke quickly spiraled out of control. Newspapers reported the story, historians cited it, and it even made its way into history textbooks. It became a widely accepted "fact," much like a game of telephone that ended with Fillmore being remembered for bathtubs instead of, say, the Compromise of 1850.

Picture Fillmore's ghost roaming the White House, hearing tourists whisper, "Hey, isn't he the president who installed the first bathtub?" You can almost imagine him groaning, "Really? That's my legacy?"

To make matters even funnier, people genuinely celebrated Fillmore as a hygiene hero, believing he had revolutionized bathing in the White House. Mencken later admitted the entire story was fabricated, but by then, it was too late—the legend had stuck.

"Really? That's my legacy?"

So, while Fillmore's presidency might not be remembered for much else, his fabricated role as "America's bathtub president" remains a humorous legacy that far outlasted his real-life policies.

Franklin Pierce, the 14th president of the United States, may not be the most famous of his era, but his time in office wasn't without its share of lighthearted moments. One particularly amusing story highlights Pierce's clumsiness and a playful encounter at a White House event.

In 1853, shortly after becoming president, Pierce hosted a gathering that included members of Congress and their families. Among the guests were several young girls eager to meet him. Known for his approachable nature, Pierce decided to join the children in a spontaneous game of tag. The scene must have been a sight—giggling girls darting around the grand halls, hiding behind furniture, while the president, dressed in his formal attire, chased after them.

What started as a joyful game took a humorous twist when Pierce misjudged a step near the staircase. In a slapstick moment, he tripped over his own feet and tumbled down the stairs, arms flailing. The girls gasped, but their shock quickly turned into laughter as they watched the president, momentarily disheveled but unhurt.

Without missing a beat, Pierce stood up, dusted off his suit, and, with a grin, joked, "Well, I suppose I can't catch you all if I'm down here!" His good-natured remark sent the children into fits of giggles, and even the adults couldn't help but laugh at the sight of their president embracing the playful moment.

Rather than feeling embarrassed, Pierce continued to play along, joining the girls in a game of follow-the-leader. This lighthearted episode reveals the softer side of Pierce's presidency, showing that even in the midst of political challenges, there's always room for laughter and human connection.

James Buchanan
1857-1861

Buchanan was known for hosting lavish dinner parties at the White House, but his fondness for a humble dish, "cabbage and pickled pork," became an unexpected source of amusement. Buchanan requested this meal so frequently that it became his signature dish at official dinners. During one state dinner, amidst the fancy fare, Buchanan once again asked for his beloved cabbage. While the request seemed innocent enough, the press seized on this unusual preference for such a simple food.

Before long, the media began calling him "Old Buck and His Cabbage," a nickname that quickly spread through Washington and across the nation. At a time when presidents were expected to embody refinement and class, the idea of the nation's leader enjoying cabbage became a subject of gossip and lighthearted ridicule. Political cartoonists ran with the joke, depicting Buchanan surrounded by oversized cabbages, turning his favorite dish into a national running gag.

Instead of being offended or embarrassed, Buchanan embraced the humor. He continued serving cabbage at White House dinners and reportedly laughed along with the public's reaction. Rather than shy away from the teasing, Buchanan took it in stride, proudly telling his guests that the dish represented his simple, frugal roots in Pennsylvania.

This story highlights Buchanan's ability to laugh at himself and find joy in life's lighter moments. In a role filled with serious responsibilities, his willingness to embrace the cabbage joke shows the value of not taking oneself too seriously.

Sometimes, even a president can be remembered for something as humble—and funny—as a love of cabbage!

Abraham Lincoln
1861-1865

Abraham Lincoln, the 16th president of the United States, is celebrated for his leadership during the Civil War and his wisdom, but he's also remembered for his sharp sense of humor. One particularly funny story from Lincoln's presidency took place at a White House event in 1862.

During a gathering of officials and diplomats, Lincoln, known for his storytelling, decided to lighten the mood with one of his famous tales. He began by recounting an experience from his days as a young rail-splitter in Illinois, which quickly became more comical than expected.

Lincoln described a day when he encountered a bear cub while walking in the woods. Instead of being afraid, he decided to chase the cub. With his arms flailing, Lincoln reenacted his awkward pursuit, but the humor intensified when he explained how he slipped and fell into a mud puddle during the chase. The audience was already laughing, but the best was yet to come.

Lincoln then claimed that after his muddy fall, the cub's mother appeared. In a panic, he "remembered the most important thing" and shouted, "I'm a vegetarian!" The absurdity of Lincoln yelling at a bear about his diet had the room in stitches.

As he stood up to finish the story, Lincoln mimicked his exaggerated escape, waving his long arms wildly and grinning as the audience roared with laughter. His final punchline—"And that's why I always carry a stick when I go camping!"—left even the most serious diplomats laughing uncontrollably.

This story reveals Lincoln's unique ability to use humor to connect with others, even during a time of national crisis. His storytelling not only lightened the atmosphere but also showcased his approachable and witty personality, proving that even a president could enjoy a good laugh.

Andrew Johnson
1865-1869

Andrew Johnson, the 17th President of the United States, was known for his fiery personality, stubbornness, and, at times, lack of social grace. While his presidency is often remembered for the challenges of Reconstruction and his impeachment, one particularly humorous story from his time as Vice President stands out.

The date was March 4, 1865—Inauguration Day. Abraham Lincoln had just been re-elected, and the Civil War was nearing its end. Lincoln, renowned for his eloquence, was set to deliver a powerful second inaugural address focused on healing a divided nation. However, before Lincoln took the stage, newly-elected Vice President Andrew Johnson had to deliver his own address, which would go down in history for all the wrong reasons.

The day before, Johnson had been feeling unwell, likely due to fatigue and stress. To settle his nerves, he was advised to drink whiskey. Unfortunately, Johnson, unaccustomed to alcohol, drank too much. By the time he arrived for his swearing-in, he was visibly intoxicated.

As Johnson began speaking, it became clear something was wrong. Slurring his words and swaying, his speech—intended to be brief and ceremonial— quickly turned into a rambling, incoherent monologue. He boasted about his humble beginnings and compared himself to working men across the nation, all while stumbling over his words. At one point, he addressed members of the Cabinet by name, urging them to stay loyal to Lincoln.

What should have been a formal, dignified moment became an awkward and embarrassing spectacle. Some in the crowd cringed, while others couldn't suppress their laughter. Lincoln watched in horror, surely regretting choosing Johnson as his running mate.

Though Johnson's drunken tirade was widely criticized at the time, it has since become a humorous reminder that even the most serious occasions can be disrupted by unexpected—and sometimes entertaining—mishaps.

Ulysses S. Grant
1869-1877

Ulysses S. Grant, the 18th President of the United States, is remembered for his military prowess, but his presidency had its share of lighthearted moments. One of the most amusing stories centers around his disregard for speed limits—particularly when riding horses.

Grant, an avid horseman with a natural talent for handling horses, continued his passion during his presidency. He often took fast rides around Washington, D.C., where strict speed regulations were enforced for horse-drawn carriages to protect pedestrians. Unfortunately for Grant, his love of speed often got him into trouble.

In the 1870s, during one of his brisk rides, Grant was stopped by Washington police officer William H. West for speeding. Officer West, unaware he was speaking to the president, sternly warned Grant about the dangers of riding too fast. Grant, known for his quiet demeanor, apologized and promised to slow down.

However, the very next day, Officer West caught Grant speeding again. This time, West recognized the president but didn't hesitate to perform his duty. With a mix of humor and professionalism, he told Grant, "I am very sorry, Mr. President, but duty is duty, and I will have to place you under arrest."

Amused by the situation and impressed by West's commitment to the law, Grant didn't protest. He calmly went with the officer to the police station and paid a $20 fine—a large sum at the time, equivalent to over $600 today.

This incident became legendary, not just because a sitting U.S. president was arrested, but because of Grant's good-natured acceptance of the law. It highlighted a charming side of Grant—a leader who, despite his position, respected the rules and appreciated a little humor in the process. The story remains a delightful and humorous anecdote from Grant's presidency, showing that even the most powerful man could be held accountable.

Rutherford B. Hayes
1877-1881

Ever heard of Rutherford B. Hayes, the 19th president of the United States? He may not be the most famous name in history, but he's got one of the funniest presidential stories—trust me, it involves a goat, and it's one you won't forget.

Here's what happened: Rutherford B. Hayes was pretty laid-back compared to other presidents. He lived in the White House with his wife Lucy, their kids, and a collection of pets. One of the more unusual pets was a goat named Old Whiskers. Yes, a goat! And Old Whiskers wasn't just lounging on the White House lawn—he was part of the family. Hayes's youngest son, Scott, loved him and would hitch the goat to a small cart, riding around like he had his own personal goat-powered vehicle.

But one day, things got out of hand. Scott took Old Whiskers for a ride around the White House grounds, but this time, the goat had other plans. Instead of a peaceful stroll, Old Whiskers took off at full speed, breaking free from the White House gates and racing down Pennsylvania Avenue with Scott holding on for dear life.

The scene was pure chaos. People on the street couldn't believe what they were seeing—a runaway goat dragging a child through the streets of Washington, D.C. Some laughed, while others dodged out of the way as Old Whiskers charged forward.

Then came the best part: President Hayes heard the commotion, ran outside, and joined the chase! Picture the president, in his formal suit, sprinting down the street after a runaway goat. Eventually, White House staff and neighbors helped corral Old Whiskers and bring Scott back safely.

The story spread quickly, and soon everyone in Washington was talking about the day President Hayes chased a goat down Pennsylvania Avenue. It's a hilarious and memorable moment that shows even presidents have their "What just happened?" days!

James Garfield, the 20th president of the United States, may not be a household name, but he was at the center of one of Washington, D.C.'s most amusing stories—featuring a hilarious misunderstanding, some chickens, and a president with a great sense of humor!

Before becoming president, Garfield was a respected member of Congress, known for his intelligence and quick wit. What made him even more memorable was his love of a good joke. His easygoing nature and self-deprecating humor led to one of the funniest moments in his political career.

The story begins when a rumor circulated that Congressman Garfield had a surprising side job: running a chicken farm. At the time, politicians were expected to be serious and dignified, so the idea of a congressman raising chickens was both bizarre and amusing. The rumor spread quickly, and soon, people were whispering about "Farmer Garfield" and his supposed chicken business.

Instead of denying the rumor or getting upset, Garfield leaned into the joke. He proudly played along, boasting that his chickens were the best egg-layers in the country and claiming his farm was a thriving success. The "Farmer Garfield" persona became a running gag among his friends and colleagues.

Taking the joke further, Garfield even sent his friends packages of "eggs from his farm"—which were just regular store-bought eggs. Everyone was in on the joke, and it became a hit in Washington.

Garfield's playful attitude won him even more popularity. His ability to laugh at himself and embrace the absurd rumor showed a lighthearted side of a political figure, making him more relatable. While his presidency was tragically cut short, the "Farmer Garfield" story highlights his humor and self-awareness, proving that even presidents can turn rumors into legendary jokes.

Chester A. Arthur
1881-1885

Chester A. Arthur, the 21st president of the United States, was best known for his refined sense of style and love for high society. However, one of the funniest stories about him has nothing to do with fashion and everything to do with an unexpected encounter with a cow.

Arthur, not much of an outdoorsman, preferred tailored suits and elegant dinner parties to the rustic charms of farm life. So, when a political supporter invited him to visit their farm, it was far outside his comfort zone. Still, being a good sport, Arthur accepted the invitation.

Upon his arrival, the farmer and his family were thrilled to host the president. They eagerly showed him around, introducing him to the farm animals. To add a bit of fun, the farmer suggested that Arthur try milking a cow. Despite being entirely unprepared, Arthur graciously agreed, not wanting to offend his hosts.

Dressed in a far-too-fancy outfit for farm work, Arthur awkwardly sat beside the cow while the farmer gave him a quick lesson. As he grabbed the cow's udder and attempted to milk it, the cow, unimpressed with the president's technique, kicked the bucket right out of his hands, sending milk splashing everywhere. Arthur's elegant suit was splattered, and the overturned bucket created a scene of chaos.

The farmhands and the farmer's family couldn't contain their laughter at the sight of the sophisticated president being bested by a cow. To their surprise, Arthur laughed along with them. He saw the humor in the situation and embraced the absurdity of it all.

This amusing story of Arthur's cow mishap quickly spread and became a favorite during his presidency. It showed that even the most dignified leaders could have humbling—and hilarious—moments. Arthur's ability to laugh at himself only endeared him more to those around him.

Grover Cleveland
1885-1889

Grover Cleveland, the 22nd and 24th president of the United States, is often remembered for his serious demeanor and straightforward leadership. However, one humorous incident during his second term proves that even Cleveland couldn't escape an embarrassing, yet hilarious, moment—thanks to a prank pulled by his White House staff.

During Cleveland's second term, the mostly male staff at the White House enjoyed playing practical jokes on each other. Cleveland, always focused and work-driven, became the target of one of their best pranks. The opportunity came during one of his routine lunch breaks.

After a long day of meetings and paperwork, Cleveland was ready for his usual meal. The staff, knowing how much Cleveland valued his lunchtime routine, decided it was the perfect time to spring their joke. When the president's lunch arrived, he lifted the lid of his plate, expecting his usual meal. Instead, he found a live turtle staring back at him!

At first, Cleveland was bewildered, unsure of what to make of the turtle sitting on his plate. But after a brief moment, the absurdity of the situation hit him, and he burst out laughing. The serious, no-nonsense president couldn't help but appreciate the humor in the unexpected sight.

Far from being angry, Cleveland called in the staff, who had been nervously waiting outside. Seeing their president laughing, they knew their prank had succeeded. Instead of scolding them, Cleveland shared the moment with his staff, enjoying the break from the stresses of the presidency.

The turtle prank became legendary among White House staff, showcasing a rarely seen lighthearted side of Cleveland. Known for his tough political stances, this episode revealed that even a serious leader could enjoy a good joke—and laugh at himself. It's a reminder that even the most focused presidents need a moment of levity, and for Cleveland, that came in the form of a turtle served for lunch!

Benjamin Harrison
1889-1893

Benjamin Harrison, the 23rd president of the United States, might not be remembered for his sense of humor, but one of the funniest stories from his presidency revolves around his unintentional mishap with a new and mysterious technology: electricity.

When Harrison took office in 1889, the White House underwent a significant upgrade—electric lighting was installed for the first time, replacing the old gas lamps. This was a groundbreaking technological advancement, but Harrison wasn't thrilled. In fact, he was terrified.

Electricity was still new, and many people didn't fully understand how it worked. Rumors swirled that touching a light switch could result in an electric shock or worse. Harrison, not trusting the new technology, shared these fears. His wife, Caroline, was equally cautious. The couple refused to touch the light switches in the White House, believing the rumors and convinced they could get electrocuted.

What followed was a comical situation: instead of operating the lights themselves, the Harrisons left it to the White House staff to flip the switches. If the staff wasn't available, they would rather leave the lights on overnight than risk touching a switch. The image of the President and First Lady, too scared to turn the lights on or off, quickly became an inside joke among the staff and visitors alike.

Harrison's fear of electricity may have seemed irrational, but it added a lighthearted and human touch to his otherwise serious presidency. His cautiousness in embracing this new technology made him relatable, showing that even the most powerful people can have unexpected fears.

This story of Harrison's fear of electricity remains one of the most amusing anecdotes from his time in office, reminding us that even presidents can be spooked by new technology—and sometimes those fears can lead to the funniest moments!

William McKinley, the 25th president of the United States, was known for his calm leadership and serious demeanor. However, one of the most amusing moments of his presidency occurred during a formal White House event, which quickly turned into an unintentional comedy show due to a musical mishap.

McKinley loved music, and military bands often performed at his official receptions. During one such evening, with foreign dignitaries in attendance, a renowned military band was scheduled to play. The event was meticulously planned—except for a behind-the-scenes mistake.

In the rush to prepare, a trumpet player and a tuba player accidentally swapped instruments. Unaware of the mix-up, the bandleader gave the signal to begin. What followed was pure chaos. The tuba player, holding the tiny trumpet, struggled to hit the high notes, producing awkward squeaks. Meanwhile, the trumpet player, stuck with the oversized tuba, could only deliver deep, rumbling tones. The result was a hilariously out-of-tune performance.

At first, the guests exchanged confused glances, unsure of the odd sounds. Even McKinley, seated at the front, couldn't help but notice. Known for his reserved nature, he tried to maintain composure, but as the discordant performance continued, the situation became undeniably funny.

Soon, the entire room erupted in laughter, including McKinley. The sight of two musicians playing the wrong instruments was simply too amusing. Though the bandleader eventually stopped the performance, by then the mood had shifted from formal to lighthearted.

Rather than feel embarrassed, McKinley embraced the humor. He later recounted the "tuba-trumpet disaster" to friends, laughing at the unexpected hilarity, proving that even the most serious leaders can enjoy a good laugh when things go awry.

Theodore Roosevelt
1901-1909

Theodore Roosevelt, the 26th president of the United States, was famous for his adventurous spirit and bold personality. One of the most amusing and well-known stories about him involves an unexpected encounter with a bear during a hunting trip in 1902, showcasing both his toughness and sense of fairness.

On a bear hunting expedition in Mississippi, Roosevelt and his group had no luck finding a bear after hours of searching. Determined to help, the guides tracked down an old, exhausted bear, tied it to a tree, and suggested Roosevelt take the shot.

To everyone's surprise, Roosevelt refused. Though an experienced hunter, he found it unfair to shoot a defenseless animal, declaring it unsportsmanlike. He insisted the bear be set free, saying he couldn't bring himself to kill a creature that had no chance to escape.

The news spread quickly, and the press loved the story. Cartoonists began sketching Roosevelt with a small bear, and his compassionate decision captured the public's imagination. The incident even inspired the creation of the "Teddy bear," a stuffed toy named after Roosevelt's nickname, "Teddy."

The contrast between Roosevelt's rugged persona—known for leading soldiers in battle and his love of the wilderness—and the cute, cuddly toy named after him was both funny and heartwarming. The same man who once gave a speech after being shot by an assassin became forever linked to a beloved children's toy.

Roosevelt's refusal to shoot the bear highlighted his sense of fairness, turning a hunting trip into one of the most charming stories of his presidency. Millions of children have since grown up with a "Teddy bear," a lasting symbol of Roosevelt's unexpected kindness.

William Howard Taft
1909-1913

William Howard Taft, the 27th president of the United States, is remembered for many things, but one of the most amusing stories from his time involves a baseball game and a tradition that lives on today—throwing out the first pitch.

In 1910, Taft was invited to attend the Washington Senators' Opening Day game, marking the start of a tradition that many presidents have since followed. Taft, an avid baseball fan, was thrilled to take part. When he arrived at the stadium, the crowd was excited to see him, but they had no idea they were witnessing the birth of a new tradition.

As the game was about to begin, Taft was handed a baseball and asked to throw the ceremonial first pitch. He stood, waved to the crowd, and tossed the ball toward the field. While it might not have been the most perfect pitch, it was the first time a president threw out a first pitch at a Major League Baseball game, starting a tradition that continues to this day.

But the real humor came later in the game. Taft, a large man, had been sitting in a wooden chair for quite some time and started to feel uncomfortable. Wanting to stretch his legs, he stood up without intending to cause a scene. However, when the president stood, the entire crowd followed suit, thinking it was part of the event. When Taft sat back down, the crowd did too.

This unintentional act became what we now call the "seventh-inning stretch," where fans stand and stretch during baseball games. What began as a simple stretch by the president turned into one of baseball's most beloved traditions.

For teens today, the idea of a president accidentally starting a sports tradition is both hilarious and relatable. Taft's need for a break shows that even leaders have their casual moments, and sometimes traditions start with something as simple as standing up to stretch!

Woodrow Wilson
1913-1921

Woodrow Wilson, the 28th president of the United States, is remembered for his leadership during World War I and his serious demeanor. However, one of the most hilarious moments of his presidency occurred on a simple train ride, revealing a more lighthearted side of Wilson.

Wilson often traveled by train for meetings and speeches. On one such trip, he decided to take a nap in his private car, unaware of the surprise visitor about to disrupt his rest.

At a stop, a curious goat somehow boarded the train and wandered into Wilson's car while he slept. The president, unaware, was jolted awake by a strange noise. Opening his eyes, he found himself face-to-face with the goat, happily munching on papers left on the table.

Startled, Wilson tried to shoo the goat away, but the mischievous animal wasn't leaving quietly. The goat darted around the small compartment, knocking over papers and causing mayhem. Wilson, known for his calm and intellectual nature, suddenly found himself chasing the goat, trying in vain to catch it.

By the time his staff arrived to help, the scene was pure chaos. Papers flew everywhere, and the usually composed president was in a full-blown chase with the stubborn goat. After some effort, the staff captured the animal, leaving Wilson disheveled but laughing at the absurdity of the situation.

This story became a favorite among Wilson's staff, who loved the image of their serious boss being outwitted by a goat. It's a reminder that even presidents find themselves in ridiculous situations—and sometimes, all you can do is laugh.

Warren G. Harding
1921-1923

Warren G. Harding, the 29th president of the United States, was known for his laid-back personality, and one of the funniest moments of his presidency occurred during a public speaking event. Harding, who enjoyed social gatherings and casual interactions, was delivering a speech at an outdoor rally that quickly took an unexpectedly humorous turn.

On a sunny afternoon, hundreds gathered to hear Harding speak. As he stepped up to the podium, the crowd was eager to listen. However, as he began his speech, a fly landed right on his forehead, just above his eyebrows.

At first, the audience tried to stay focused on Harding's words, but the fly quickly became the star of the show. Unaware of the insect, Harding continued speaking confidently while the fly casually strolled across his forehead. The crowd, trying not to laugh, watched as it made its way toward his nose.

By the time the fly reached Harding's upper lip, the audience was struggling to contain their giggles. Harding, still oblivious, paused when he noticed the crowd's amusement. Confused, he wiped his face and finally swatted the fly away with an exaggerated motion.

The audience erupted in laughter, and Harding, realizing what had happened, laughed along with them. With a grin, he joked, "Well, I guess that fly had something to say!" His good-natured response turned an awkward moment into a memorable and funny one.

Harding's ability to laugh at himself endeared him to the crowd, and the speech continued in high spirits. This story reminds us that even during serious occasions, unexpected moments can bring humor—and sometimes, the best thing to do is simply laugh it off.

Calvin Coolidge
1923-1929

Calvin Coolidge, the 30th president of the United States, is often remembered for his quiet, reserved nature, earning him the nickname "Silent Cal." Despite his serious demeanor, one famous story reveals his playful sense of humor and sharp wit, proving even the most stoic leaders can deliver a well-timed joke.

The story takes place at a White House dinner party where Coolidge, known for speaking very little, intrigued his fellow guests with his reticence. A woman seated next to him, eager to challenge his reputation, made a bold bet with her friends. She claimed she could get Coolidge to say more than three words during dinner.

Determined to win, the woman turned to the president and confidently said, "Mr. Coolidge, I made a bet with my friends that I could get you to say more than three words tonight." Expecting him to engage in conversation or at least offer a polite reply, she awaited his response.

Coolidge, however, wasn't one to miss an opportunity for humor. Without missing a beat, he looked at her and simply replied, "You lose."

The woman was taken aback, and the entire table erupted in laughter. Coolidge, true to his "Silent Cal" nickname, had spoken—just two words—and with them, he had won the moment. His dry wit had not only upheld his reputation but also created one of the most memorable and humorous moments of his presidency.

This story perfectly captures Coolidge's understated cleverness. While he wasn't known for grand speeches, his ability to deliver humor with precision showed that sometimes, less is more. His quick, witty response proves that even the quietest people can leave the strongest impressions, and Coolidge's well-timed humor became an unforgettable part of his legacy.

Herbert Hoover
1929-1933

Herbert Hoover, the 31st president of the United States, is often remembered as a serious figure, but one hilarious incident from his presidency proves that even he wasn't immune to moments of pure awkwardness. This particular tale involves a comical encounter with a rather unruly turkey, just before Thanksgiving.

In the early 1930s, it was customary for the president to receive a live turkey as a gift ahead of the holiday. The bird was intended to be the centerpiece of the presidential Thanksgiving feast. However, when Hoover was in office, things didn't go as planned. One year, the White House was presented with a particularly feisty turkey, far from the docile bird they expected.

During the presentation, with Hoover and a crowd of onlookers admiring the turkey, the bird suddenly broke free from its handler. Flapping its wings and gobbling loudly, the turkey dashed across the White House lawn, creating absolute chaos. In an effort to maintain his composure, Hoover attempted to help catch the runaway bird, but his approach only made things worse. As he neared the turkey, the bird made a bold move and charged directly at the president!

The sight of the President of the United States being chased around the lawn by a large, frantic turkey left everyone in stitches. Hoover, dodging the bird's wild movements, couldn't help but laugh at the absurdity of the situation. Eventually, the staff managed to wrangle the turkey, but not before it earned the title of the most rambunctious bird in White House history.

The turkey chase became the talk of the White House, and Hoover himself chuckled at the memory of being pursued by his own Thanksgiving dinner. This story is a reminder that even in formal settings, things can go hilariously wrong. Hoover's turkey incident shows that no one, not even a president, is immune to life's unexpected moments of humor.

Franklin D. Roosevelt
1933-1945

Franklin D. Roosevelt, or FDR, the 32nd president of the United States, is best known for his leadership during the Great Depression and World War II. However, amidst the gravity of his presidency, he had his fair share of lighthearted moments. One of the funniest stories involves a clever prank that left FDR speechless and laughing.

FDR was a fan of practical jokes, enjoying the opportunity to lighten the mood in the White House despite the immense pressures he faced. On one particular day, a mischievous staff member decided to play a prank on the president using an unexpected item: a rubber chicken.

The setup was simple yet brilliant. FDR frequently hosted formal meals with important guests, and the White House kitchen staff was used to preparing elaborate feasts. But this time, they had something different in mind for dessert—an oversized, perfectly cooked rubber chicken.

As the meal progressed, FDR conversed with his guests, unaware of the prank unfolding. When it came time for the "main course" to be served, the staff presented the rubber chicken on a silver platter, just as they would with any gourmet dish. The guests, all in on the joke, eagerly watched as FDR reached for the carving knife.

When FDR attempted to cut into the chicken, he quickly realized something wasn't right. The chicken was unusually firm. His confusion turned to amusement as he discovered it was made of rubber. Bursting into laughter, FDR held up the fake chicken and quipped, "Well, I've had all sorts of meals here, but this takes the cake!"

The entire table erupted in laughter, and the story of the rubber chicken became a favorite around the White House. Rather than being upset, FDR embraced the joke and often retold it with a smile. This moment revealed that, even in the toughest times, the president could appreciate a good laugh, proving that humor can brighten even the darkest of days.

Harry S. Truman
1945-1953

Harry S. Truman, the 33rd president of the United States, was known for his no-nonsense approach to leadership, but one of the funniest and most awkward moments of his presidency involved a comical mishap with an elevator in the White House.

One evening, after hosting a dinner for foreign diplomats and politicians, Truman decided to head back to his private quarters for some rest. Like any president, he opted to take the White House elevator. However, this wasn't your typical elevator—it was an old, temperamental one that seemed to have a mind of its own.

As Truman stepped inside and closed the door, he pressed the button to go upstairs. But nothing happened. He pressed the button again. Still nothing. Confused, he tried to open the door, but it wouldn't budge. The president was stuck.

At first, Truman thought it was just a minor glitch, but as time went on, he realized he was truly trapped. Unable to call for help, he did what anyone would do in that situation—he began banging on the elevator door, hoping someone would hear him.

Hearing the noise, White House staff rushed over, unsure of what was happening. When they realized the president was stuck in the elevator, they quickly began trying to free him. But just as they were about to open the door, the elevator suddenly started moving on its own, stopping one floor below Truman's intended destination.

When the door finally opened, a slightly frustrated but amused Truman stepped out. Dusting off his jacket, he grinned and quipped, "Well, that was an unexpected stop!"

Truman's ability to laugh at the situation reflected his down-to-earth nature. This story serves as a reminder that even the most powerful leaders face unexpected situations—and sometimes, the best thing to do is laugh and roll with it.

Dwight D. Eisenhower
1953-1961

One of the funniest stories about Dwight D. Eisenhower, the 34th president of the United States, revolves around his deep love for golf. Eisenhower was an avid golfer, often playing to unwind and clear his mind.

His passion for the game was so strong that he even had a putting green installed on the White House lawn. However, it was his battles on the course that made for some of the most memorable moments, particularly with one pesky tree.

Eisenhower was a member of the Augusta National Golf Club, where he often played. But there was one feature of the course that drove him mad: a large pine tree standing on the 17th hole. This tree, which would later become known as the "Eisenhower Tree," had an uncanny ability to block his shots, repeatedly ruining his game.

Frustrated, Eisenhower frequently complained about the tree. In 1956, during a club meeting, he reached his limit and stood up to propose the tree's removal, citing its interference with his shots. What followed was both humorous and diplomatic.

Clifford Roberts, the club's chairman, recognized that cutting down a beloved tree wouldn't sit well with the members. But rather than directly opposing the President, Roberts quickly adjourned the meeting, declaring the topic off-limits.

Despite Eisenhower's repeated grumbling, the tree stayed. It became a legend at Augusta, with members joking that even the President of the United States couldn't win this battle.

The story highlights Eisenhower's human side, showing that even the most powerful leader in the world had to contend with life's small annoyances— like a stubborn tree messing with his golf game. Sometimes, even nature gets the last laugh!

John F. Kennedy
1961-1963

One of the funniest stories about John F. Kennedy, the 35th president of the United States, comes from a comical mix-up involving a group of eager Boy Scouts. Known for his charm and quick wit, JFK had a knack for turning awkward situations into something lighthearted, and this tale captures that perfectly.

In the early 1960s, Kennedy was hosting an important international summit at the White House. The meeting was a serious affair, filled with world leaders and diplomats discussing major global issues. The atmosphere was formal, as one would expect for such high-stakes discussions.

Meanwhile, a group of Boy Scouts was visiting Washington, D.C., and had scheduled a tour of the White House. However, due to a small staff error, the Scouts were accidentally led into the middle of this critical diplomatic meeting instead of the usual public areas.

The sight of the uniformed Scouts, wide-eyed and excited, wandering into the room of serious dignitaries was both unexpected and humorous. The boys had no idea they were interrupting, and the diplomats looked baffled. But JFK, always quick to see the humor in a situation, immediately lightened the mood.

With a grin, Kennedy stood up and warmly greeted the Scouts. "Well, boys," he said with a laugh, "you've just met some of the finest leaders in the world. What do you think?" His playful remark broke the tension, and the room erupted in laughter.

JFK took a few moments to chat with the Scouts, making them feel welcome before they were gently escorted out. The Boy Scouts left with an unforgettable story, and the world leaders admired Kennedy's ability to handle the unexpected with humor and grace. This story showcases why JFK remains one of the most charismatic and approachable presidents in American history.

Lyndon B. Johnson
1963-1969

One of the funniest stories about President Lyndon B. Johnson, the 36th president of the United States, centers around his unique approach to multitasking, highlighted by the infamous "shower phone" incident. Known for his larger-than-life personality, Johnson had a habit of conducting business anytime, anywhere—and that included while getting clean.

Johnson believed in staying connected no matter what. He had telephones installed in nearly every room of the White House, including his personal bathroom. But his most unusual request came when he had a special phone installed in his shower, ensuring he could continue his presidential duties without interruption, even during his daily routine.

One day, in the midst of an important phone call with a cabinet member, Johnson decided to step into the shower. Rather than end the conversation, he carried the phone with him. However, the water from the shower soon began to cause static on the line, making it difficult to hear. Frustrated by the poor connection, Johnson started shouting at his staff to fix the issue immediately.

What made the situation even funnier was that Johnson, completely naked in his shower, was barking orders about a phone call while water splashed around him. The staff, realizing the absurdity of the situation, couldn't help but laugh.

This incident perfectly captures Johnson's quirky personality and determination to never be disconnected from his work.

Whether in the shower, the bathroom, or even on the toilet, Johnson was always on the job. The "shower phone" episode is a memorable example of how he took his presidency seriously—but never in a conventional way. It's a story that left those around him with a hilarious memory they would never forget.

Richard Nixon
1969-1973

One of the funniest stories about Richard Nixon, the 37th president of the United States, took place during his 1960 presidential campaign, when a live television mishap turned into an unexpectedly hilarious moment. Known for his serious demeanor, Nixon was running against John F. Kennedy in one of the most famous presidential races in U.S. history. However, during a campaign stop in Iowa, Nixon found himself in an awkward yet comical situation that people still talk about today.

Nixon agreed to make a live TV appearance at a county fair, aiming to show voters his down-to-earth side. The plan was simple: he would give a short speech and walk around the fairgrounds, shaking hands and interacting with the public. Things went smoothly at first—Nixon smiled, greeted farmers, and seemed at ease. Then, TV producers decided to film him with one of the farm's cows.

As Nixon approached the cow, hoping to appear relatable, something unexpected happened. Just as he got close, the cow lifted its tail and relieved itself—right in front of him! The moment was perfectly timed, and the cameras caught everything on live television. Nixon stood frozen in disbelief as the crowd erupted in laughter.

To his credit, Nixon quickly recovered with a witty remark, joking, "I guess this is what happens when you get too close to the real issues!" The crowd laughed even harder, and the footage became an instant hit.

This humorous incident showed a lighter side of Nixon, who was usually seen as serious and reserved. It became one of the most memorable moments from his campaign, proving that even in politics, sometimes the funniest moments are the least expected—like a cow's untimely contribution at a county fair.

Note: ChatGPT could not generate ANY image of Nixon or several other figures after numerous attempts.

Gerald R. Ford
1974-1977

One of the funniest stories about President Gerald R. Ford, the 38th President of the United States, centers around a memorable and very public golfing mishap. Known for being an avid golfer, Ford also had a reputation for being a bit clumsy, a trait that led to one of his most infamous moments during the 1975 Bob Hope Desert Classic in California.

The star-studded golf tournament featured famous athletes, actors, and politicians, with Ford excited to participate. However, the day took a humorous turn when Ford, known for his powerful but unpredictable swing, teed off in front of a large crowd.

As Ford swung his club with full force, the ball veered wildly off course, striking a woman in the crowd on the head. The spectators gasped as the woman fell, though she wasn't seriously hurt. Embarrassed, Ford immediately rushed over, apologizing profusely. The woman, taking it in stride, quickly forgave him, and the tournament continued.

But the mishaps weren't over. Later that day, Ford hit yet another wayward shot, this time striking a Secret Service agent who was standing nearby. Once again, Ford had to apologize for his errant golf swing.

The media had a field day with Ford's blunders, and comedians, particularly Chevy Chase on "Saturday Night Live," seized the opportunity to joke about the president's clumsiness. Ford, however, took it all in good humor, often making light of his own lack of precision on the golf course.

This story highlights Ford's ability to laugh at himself, making him more relatable to the public. His golfing mishaps remind us that even presidents have awkward moments, and a little humor can go a long way in handling life's unexpected blunders.

Jimmy Carter
1977-1981

One of the funniest and most bizarre stories from President Jimmy Carter's time in office as the 39th president involves a surprising encounter with an unlikely adversary—a rabbit! This unusual event, dubbed the "killer rabbit" incident, occurred in 1979 and has since become one of the most amusing anecdotes of his presidency.

During a peaceful fishing trip on his family's property in Georgia, Carter was paddling a small boat, enjoying the calm of the lake. It was meant to be a relaxing escape from the pressures of the presidency. However, the tranquility was soon interrupted by a strange sight—a rabbit swimming frantically toward his boat.

Rabbits aren't known for being swimmers, nor are they typically aggressive, but this one seemed determined to reach Carter. As it got closer, Carter realized the rabbit was not just swimming; it was actually trying to climb into his boat!

Startled by the odd situation, Carter grabbed an oar and splashed water at the animal, successfully scaring it away before it could board his boat. The rabbit eventually swam back to shore, but the strange encounter left Carter both puzzled and amused.

When Carter returned to the White House and shared the story with his staff, the tale quickly made its way to the press. Soon, the media was having

a field day with the idea of the President being "attacked" by a rabbit. The Washington Post even ran a cartoon depicting the humorous event, turning the bizarre moment into a nationwide joke.

Carter took the incident in stride, laughing along with the public. The "killer rabbit" story became a lighthearted reminder that even presidents can face the absurd and unexpected, showing Carter's down-to-earth and good-natured personality.

Ronald Reagan
1981-1989

One of the funniest and most memorable stories about Ronald Reagan, the 40th president of the United States, took place during his 1984 visit to London, where he had the unique opportunity to stay at Windsor Castle and go horseback riding with Queen Elizabeth II. Reagan, a horse enthusiast, was excited about the ride, but what happened during their outing turned the moment into an unforgettable, hilarious episode.

As Reagan and the Queen rode through the scenic grounds of Windsor Castle, Reagan's horse suddenly let out a loud, unmistakable noise—a horse-sized "fart." While the situation could have been awkward, both Reagan and the Queen handled it with grace and humor.

Without missing a beat, Reagan turned to the Queen and jokingly said, "I'm terribly sorry, Your Majesty!" The Queen, in her famously composed and witty manner, responded, "That's quite alright, Mr. President. I thought it was the horse!"

Their light-hearted exchange became a widely shared story, illustrating Reagan's ability to defuse embarrassing moments with humor. The Queen's quick-witted response added to the charm of the incident, making it a favorite tale that people still talk about.

This moment highlights how humor can bridge formalities, even between world leaders. It showed that, despite the grandeur of their positions, Reagan and the Queen could share a genuine laugh over an unexpected situation. For teens, this story serves as a reminder that even the most important figures experience awkward moments—and how you handle them makes all the difference.

Reagan's easygoing nature and the Queen's gracious reply turned a potentially awkward situation into one of mutual respect and laughter, proving that humor can make even the most formal encounters more enjoyable and memorable.

George H. W. Bush
1989-1993

One of the most hilarious stories from George H.W. Bush, the 41st president of the United States, took place during a White House Christmas event in 1991, involving an unexpected and comical interaction with holiday decorations. Dubbed the "Turkey Bowling" incident, it became a legendary part of Bush's time in office.

During the festive celebration, the White House was lavishly decorated, and a group of staffers and reporters had gathered for a light-hearted holiday event. As part of the fun, someone brought out a large, frozen turkey. As a joke or challenge, someone suggested they try bowling with it—using the turkey to knock down bowling pins.

Most presidents might have politely declined such a silly activity. But George H.W. Bush, known for his playful side, embraced the challenge. With a grin, Bush grabbed the frozen turkey, got into a bowling stance, and sent it sliding across the polished White House floors, aiming to knock down the pins.

The sight of the President of the United States in a suit, bowling with a frozen turkey in the White House, was both surreal and hilarious. Staffers and reporters burst into laughter as the turkey skidded along the floor, knocking over pins (and, according to some versions of the story, even taking out a few decorations).

This lighthearted moment transformed the formal White House into a temporary bowling alley, showing Bush's ability to enjoy life's simple pleasures. The "Turkey Bowling" incident became a memorable example of Bush's sense of humor and his ability to connect with others by not taking himself too seriously.

For teens, this story serves as a reminder that even in the most serious roles, finding joy and laughter is essential. Bush's playful nature during this event proves that a little fun can create lasting memories, even in the most unexpected settings.

Bill Clinton
1993-2001

One of the most memorable and humorous anecdotes involving Bill Clinton, the 42nd president of the United States, occurred during a 1995 state visit from Boris Yeltsin, the President of Russia. This incident has since become a legendary tale of diplomatic hilarity.

The night before their formal meeting, Yeltsin was staying at Blair House, the official residence for foreign dignitaries. In the early hours, Secret Service agents found him wandering along Pennsylvania Avenue in his underwear, trying to hail a cab. Reportedly intoxicated, he was insisting on a ride to a local pizza place.

Fortunately, the Secret Service intervened quickly, escorting Yeltsin back to Blair House before the situation escalated into an international incident. This comical scene of one of the world's most powerful leaders drunkenly seeking pizza became a behind-the-scenes story that brought laughter to many in Washington.

When Clinton was later asked about the incident, he chuckled, describing Yeltsin's antics as "hilarious" and highlighting the Russian leader's unpredictable nature. The two leaders shared a warm relationship, and Clinton's lighthearted response helped maintain a sense of camaraderie amid the complexities of U.S.-Russia relations.

This story illustrates Clinton's knack for handling potentially embarrassing situations with humor, defusing tension and preventing escalation. His laid-back approach to diplomacy allowed him to navigate serious matters without taking himself too seriously.

This anecdote serves as a reminder that laughter can effectively ease awkward situations and strengthen connections. Clinton's ability to embrace the absurdity of the moment demonstrates that sometimes, a good sense of humor is precisely what's needed to navigate life's unexpected challenges, even in the realm of high-stakes diplomacy.

George W. Bush
2001-2008

One of the most memorable and humorous stories involving George W. Bush, the 43rd president of the United States, took place in 2008 during a press conference in Baghdad, Iraq. The event was intended to be serious, as Bush addressed the media alongside Iraqi Prime Minister Nouri al-Maliki. However, it quickly transformed into one of the most bizarre moments in modern political history.

As Bush spoke, an Iraqi journalist named Muntadhar al-Zaidi abruptly stood up and shouted, "This is a farewell kiss from the Iraqi people, you dog!" He then threw his shoe at Bush. In Middle Eastern culture, throwing a shoe is a profound insult, making the act even more striking. What made the incident comical was Bush's swift reaction; he ducked just in time, and the shoe flew over his head. A second shoe followed, and Bush dodged it with equal agility.

Amid the chaos, as security tackled the journalist, Bush remained remarkably unfazed, grinning as the room settled down. He turned the awkward moment into a lighthearted one, shrugging and quipping, "If you want the facts, it was a size 10 shoe." This remark sparked laughter from the crowd, and Bush continued the press conference as if nothing had happened.

The incident quickly went viral, with videos spreading across the internet and late-night comedians having a field day. Many praised Bush for his calm and humorous response, which defused a potentially embarrassing situation.

This story highlights the importance of handling unexpected challenges with humor. Bush's ability to turn an insult into a joke exemplifies resilience and the power of laughter to ease tension. Whether facing verbal barbs or literal shoes, maintaining composure and humor can transform difficult moments into lighter ones.

Barack Obama
2008-2016

One of the funniest moments from Barack Obama, the 44th president of the United States, occurred during the 2014 White House Easter Egg Roll. This annual event is a festive occasion for families, featuring games, music, and, of course, the traditional rolling of Easter eggs on the White House lawn. That year, Obama took part in a way that transformed a lighthearted activity into a memorable comedy routine.

As the event unfolded, Obama mingled with children and joined in the festivities. He found himself on a basketball court where kids were shooting hoops, and confident in his athletic skills, he decided to showcase his basketball prowess. Known for being a decent player, Obama stepped up to take a shot. However, things quickly went awry. His first shot missed. No problem—he shrugged it off and tried again. Then he missed again. And again.

As he continued to miss shot after shot, the situation became increasingly comical. Children, parents, and staffers watched in disbelief as the president, usually so composed, struggled with what should have been easy baskets. Instead of feeling embarrassed, Obama embraced the hilarity of the moment. With a big grin, he quipped, "I'm just warming up," and kept shooting, laughing at himself as the crowd erupted in laughter.

Even Michelle Obama, observing from the sidelines, couldn't help but chuckle at her husband's misfortunes. Eventually, he finally made a shot, and the crowd cheered as if he had just won a championship.

This story highlights the importance of maintaining a sense of humor in the face of failure. Obama's basketball mishap demonstrates that it's perfectly okay to laugh at yourself. Sometimes, the most memorable moments arise from unexpected challenges, and rolling with the punches, as he did, can turn a setback into a joyful experience.

Donald Trump
2017-2020

One of the funniest moments involving Donald Trump, the 45th president of the United States, occurred during the 2018 White House Thanksgiving turkey pardon. This annual event, where the president "pardons" a turkey, sparing it from the holiday dinner, took on a particularly amusing tone that year due to Trump's playful interactions with his family.

Traditionally, Trump was set to pardon two turkeys named Peas and Carrots. As he stood with his son Barron by his side, he delivered a speech filled with his characteristic humor. He joked about how Peas and Carrots had participated in a "fair and open election" to determine which turkey would be pardoned, quipping that despite Carrots' loss, the bird still "refused to concede and demanded a recount."

The absurdity of applying election humor to turkeys made the moment especially entertaining, and the crowd couldn't help but chuckle at the playful jab at the contentious nature of politics. Barron, however, provided a contrasting reaction. At just 12 years old, he stood beside his dad looking bored and slightly embarrassed, as if he were accustomed to his father's theatrical speeches.

As Trump continued his jokes about the turkeys, Barron's neutral expression —almost wishing he were anywhere else—caught the attention of the media. This contrast between Trump's enthusiastic antics and Barron's "too cool for this" demeanor quickly turned into a meme on social media, resonating with many teens and families who related to the awkwardness.

This moment reminds us that even presidential families experience relatable humor and awkwardness. It showcases a down-to-earth side of the Trump family, revealing that no matter how high-profile you are, you can still have those goofy, uncomfortable moments that everyone can identify with.

Joe Biden
2020-2024

One of the most touching and funny stories involving Joe Biden and his late son Beau happened when Joe shared a family moment from their time in the Senate. Beau, who was deeply admired by his father and many others, had a great sense of humor, which often brought light to Joe's busy and serious political life.

During a campaign event, Biden recounted a story about Beau from when his kids were much younger. Joe had a long commute back and forth between Washington, D.C., and Delaware, often taking the train to ensure he could spend evenings with his family.

One night, after a long day of Senate work, Biden finally made it home, tired but happy to see his sons, Beau and Hunter.

Joe told the crowd how he had sat down at the dinner table, exhausted, when Beau, who was just a boy at the time, suddenly looked at him and said, "Dad, you're home late again. What do you actually *do* in Washington all day?"

Joe, trying to explain his work in simple terms, said, "Well, Beau, I help make laws." Without skipping a beat, young Beau shot back, "Can't you make them faster so you can be home earlier?"

The crowd burst into laughter, and Joe himself chuckled at the memory. It was one of those classic, innocent kid moments that made everyone smile, and it was clear that Beau had always been able to bring humor into serious situations, even at a young age.

This story highlights the human side of politics and family life. No matter how important a job may seem, family moments and kids' humor can bring everything into perspective.

Beau's quick wit and his close relationship with his dad show that behind every public figure, there are real, funny, and heartwarming family experiences that everyone can relate to.

Think you know everything about our nation's leaders? Test your knowledge with this fun, quirky quiz! One question for each president—see how many you can get right, then check your answers without going to the back of the book. No cheating!

―――――――――――

1. **George Washington**

Known for his meticulous attention to detail, once had a wardrobe malfunction before an important meeting. What was the nature of this mishap?

A) He wore his uniform backwards and didn't realize until halfway through the meeting.
B) His wig fell off mid-speech, and he caught it just in time with his sword.
C) He had to wear an ill-fitting pair of pants that were too short, leaving his socks on full display.
D) He forgot his shoes and showed up in his horse-riding boots with spurs jangling.

Best Answer: C But hey, even the first president had his fashion faux pas!

2. John Adams

His horseback ride to his own inauguration wasn't exactly presidential. What made his journey so memorable?

A) He got lost and accidentally rode into a farmer's field, mistaking it for Philadelphia.
B) He showed up looking like a grumpy cowboy, sweaty and exhausted after a rough ride.
C) His horse threw him off right in front of the inauguration crowd, and he had to walk the rest of the way.
D) He tried to impress the crowd by galloping in, but ended up falling into a puddle instead.

Best Answer: B Who knew becoming president involved so much saddle soreness?

3. Thomas Jefferson

What strange action did Thomas Jefferson take to win a debate with European scientists about the size of American animals?

A) He dressed up as a moose and paraded around the French countryside.
B) He shipped a full-sized stuffed moose across the Atlantic to France.
C) He imported a live moose and let it loose in the gardens of Versailles.
D) He built a giant moose statue in his Paris apartment.

Best Answer: B That's one way to win an argument—by sending a moose on a diplomatic mission!

4. James Madison

How did James Madison accidentally start a fashion trend?

A) He wore a toga to a state dinner, insisting it was "classically American."
B) He refused to wear the popular tight breeches and instead showed up in loose trousers, causing a stir.
C) He wore his nightgown to a formal event, claiming it was more comfortable than a suit.
D) He accessorized his outfit with a large feathered hat that became all the rage.

Best Answer: B Madison made comfy pants cool before it was cool!

5. James Monroe

What happened when James Monroe hosted a public Fourth of July reception at the White House in 1820?

A) He turned the White House into a dance club with live music and fireworks.
B) Thousands of people showed up, ate everything, and turned the event into a chaotic food riot.
C) He accidentally scheduled the party on the wrong date and no one showed up.
D) He cooked all the food himself and won a cooking competition against his guests.

Best Answer: B Monroe's party went from presidential to pandemonium really quickly!

6. John Quincy Adams

How did journalist Anne Royall manage to secure an interview with President John Quincy Adams?

A) She disguised herself as a butler and snuck into the White House.
B) She bribed his secretary with a basket of muffins.
C) She grabbed his clothes while he was skinny-dipping in the Potomac River and refused to return them until he agreed to the interview.
D) She tricked him by pretending to be a diplomat from a foreign country.

Best Answer: C It's not every day a president is caught in such a "bare" negotiation!)

7. Andrew Jackson

What unexpected event occurred at Andrew Jackson's funeral?
A) His horse accidentally knocked over the casket during the procession.
B) His pet parrot, Poll, started loudly cursing, disrupting the service.
C) Jackson's ghost allegedly appeared and gave a speech.
D) A guest at the funeral tried to duel with another attendee over seating.

Best Answer: B Only Andrew Jackson could have a funeral upstaged by a foul-mouthed bird!

8. Martin Van Buren

How did Martin Van Buren accidentally help popularize the term "O.K."?

A) He used it in a speech and misspelled it as "O.K." instead of "okay."
B) His campaign tried to make "O.K." stand for "Old Kinderhook" to make him seem cool, but it backfired and became a joke.
C) He invented "O.K." as a secret code for his supporters to use during rallies.
D) He wrote it on all of his official documents as a personal signature.

Best Answer: B Van Buren may not have won re-election, but he did leave us with one of the most popular slang terms in history!

9. William Harry Harrison

What infamous mistake did William Henry Harrison make on his inauguration day that led to the shortest presidency in U.S. history?

A) He accidentally insulted Congress during his speech, leading to a mass walkout.
B) He forgot his speech entirely and had to improvise for two hours in the cold.
C) He gave a two-hour speech in freezing rain without wearing a coat, caught pneumonia, and died 31 days later.
D) He tried to ride a horse into the Capitol building as a show of strength and fell off.

Best Answer: C Sometimes, it's better to keep your speech—and your exposure to the elements—short!

10. John Tyler

What wild and hilarious activity took place during John Tyler's presidency, thanks to his children?

A) They turned the White House into a zoo by adopting dozens of exotic animals.
B) They held goat races inside the White House, using goats to pull them around in carts.
C) They set up an obstacle course in the Oval Office and invited foreign diplomats to participate.
D) They threw pies at each other during important state dinners.

Best Answer: B Nothing says presidential like goat-powered chaos in the halls of the White House!

11. James K. Polk

What earned James K. Polk the reputation of being "the least fun president"?

A) He refused to attend any social events and spent all his time in his office.
B) He banned dancing, card games, and even music from White House functions.
C) He threw the shortest parties in presidential history, lasting no more than 15 minutes.
D) He once fired his staff for suggesting a holiday party.

Best Answer: B Polk turned the White House into the ultimate "no-fun zone," proving that even presidents can be party poopers!

12. Zackary Taylor

What made Zachary Taylor's inauguration one of the strangest in U.S. history?

A) He gave the longest inaugural speech on record, and no one could stay awake.
B) He skipped the rehearsal, gave an extremely short speech, and refused to be sworn in on a Sunday.
C) He accidentally swore in his vice president instead of himself.
D) He delivered his entire speech in military code, confusing the audience.

Best Answer: B Taylor's laid-back attitude made for an inauguration no one would forget—especially the part where he left the country without a president for a day!

13. Millard Fillmore

What bizarre, made-up story about Millard Fillmore has hilariously stuck with him over the years?

A) He invented the first rubber duck and made it mandatory for all bathtubs.
B) He heroically installed the first bathtub in the White House, solving a national hygiene crisis.

C) He created a law requiring all government officials to take weekly baths.
D) He turned the White House into a luxury spa for visiting dignitaries.

Best Answer: B This totally fabricated story was so believable, people thought Fillmore was America's hygiene hero!

14. Franklin Pierce

What humorous mishap happened to President Franklin Pierce during a White House gathering with young girls?

A) He accidentally knocked over a priceless vase while playing catch.
B) He tripped and tumbled down a staircase while playing tag with the girls.
C) He got stuck in a White House closet while playing hide-and-seek.
D) He tried to perform a magic trick but set his sleeve on fire.

Best Answer: B Pierce's clumsy fall became a lighthearted moment that had everyone laughing!

15. James Buchanan

What humorous nickname did James Buchanan earn because of his love for a particular dish?

A) "The Pork President"
B) "Old Buck and His Cabbage"
C) "Cabbage Commander"
D) "The Pickled Pork Patriot"

Best Answer: B Buchanan's love for cabbage became a running joke in Washington, but he embraced it with pride!

16. Abraham Lincoln

What funny punchline did Abraham Lincoln deliver after telling a story about encountering a bear?

A) "And that, my friends, is why I never leave home without a rifle!"
B) "And that's how I invented bear wrestling."
C) "And that, my friends, is why I always carry a stick when I go camping!"
D) "And from that day on, I became a professional bear tamer."

Best Answer: C Lincoln's humor and storytelling had his audience laughing, even while recounting a close encounter with a bear!

What was Lincoln's belief about his Gettysburg Address after he delivered it?

A) He thought it was too short and would be forgotten.
B) He was confident it would become one of his most famous speeches.
C) He believed it was too long and boring for the audience.
D) He forgot he even gave the speech.

Best Answer: A Lincoln underestimated the impact of his brief but powerful speech, which became the most celebrated short speech in U.S. history.

17. Andrew Johnson

What memorable mishap occurred during Andrew Johnson's Vice Presidential inaugural address?

A) He accidentally recited the wrong speech, meant for a different event.
B) He became visibly intoxicated and delivered a rambling, incoherent speech.
C) He tripped on the stage and knocked over the podium.
D) He forgot Lincoln's name and called him "President What's-His-Face."

Best Answer: B Johnson's tipsy tirade became one of the most awkward and unforgettable moments in inaugural history!

18. U.S. Grant

What humorous incident involving Ulysses S. Grant occurred during his presidency?

A) He accidentally raced his horse into a public fountain during a parade.
B) He was arrested for speeding on his horse in D.C., and paid a fine.
C) He organized an impromptu horse race on the White House lawn with his Cabinet members.
D) He challenged a police officer to a race after being caught speeding.

Best Answer: B Grant's love for fast riding led to this legendary moment where even the president wasn't above the law!

19. Rutherford B. Hayes

What hilarious incident involving President Rutherford B. Hayes and his pet goat, Old Whiskers, became legendary?

A) Old Whiskers chewed up the White House lawn during a state dinner.
B) Old Whiskers ran away, pulling Hayes's son down Pennsylvania Avenue, while the president chased after them.
C) Old Whiskers accidentally knocked over a foreign diplomat during a meeting in the Oval Office.
D) Old Whiskers got stuck in a White House chandelier and had to be rescued.

Best Answer: B Imagine the president in his suit, running after a runaway goat—now that's a memorable day in history!

20. James Garfield

What humorous rumor about James Garfield did he playfully embrace while serving in Congress?

A) That he was secretly a professional magician performing at local events.
B) That he was running a chicken farm on the side to make ends meet.
C) That he operated a bakery in his spare time, specializing in pies.
D) That he had a secret talent for competitive sheep herding.

Best Answer: B Garfield even sent friends "eggs from his farm," playing along with the joke about his fictional chicken business!)

21. Chester A. Arthur

What funny incident occurred when President Chester A. Arthur visited a farm?

A) He tried to ride a pig and ended up in the mud.
B) He attempted to milk a cow, but the cow kicked over the bucket, splashing him with milk.
C) He got stuck in a chicken coop while collecting eggs.
D) He mistook a goat for a horse and tried to saddle it.

Best Answer: B Arthur's fancy suit didn't save him from this hilarious farm mishap!

22. & 24. Grover Cleveland

What hilarious prank did White House staff play on President Grover Cleveland during his lunch?

A) They replaced his meal with a rubber chicken.
B) They served him a plate with a live turtle instead of his usual lunch.
C) They swapped his coffee with vinegar as a joke.
D) They filled his soup bowl with confetti instead of food.

Best Answer: B Cleveland's good-natured reaction made this prank a legendary moment in the White House!

23. Benjamin Harrison

What comical fear did President Benjamin Harrison have during his time in the White House?

A) He thought the telephone could spy on him and refused to use it.
B) He was terrified of touching the new electric light switches, fearing he'd be shocked.
C) He refused to use the elevator, believing it might trap him.
D) He avoided mirrors, thinking they could steal his soul.

Best Answer: B Harrison's fear of electricity led him to leave the job of flipping the switches to the White House staff!

25. William McKinley

What musical mishap occurred during a formal White House event under President William McKinley?

A) The band accidentally played "Yankee Doodle" instead of the national anthem.
B) A trumpet player and a tuba player accidentally swapped instruments, resulting in an out-of-tune performance.
C) The bandleader conducted the entire performance without realizing his baton was missing.
D) A violinist dropped his bow and tried to continue playing with his fingers.

Best Answer: B The hilarious musical disaster had President McKinley and the guests laughing through the event!

26. Theodore Roosevelt

What famous event during a hunting trip led to the creation of the "Teddy bear"?

A) Roosevelt tamed a wild bear and kept it as a pet.
B) Roosevelt refused to shoot a bear that had been tied to a tree, saying it wasn't fair.
C) Roosevelt caught a bear with his bare hands and released it unharmed.
D) Roosevelt taught a bear to play fetch, amusing his hunting party.

Best Answer: B This act of kindness inspired the creation of the beloved "Teddy bear," named after Roosevelt!

27. William Howard Taft

What accidental tradition did President William Howard Taft start at a Major League Baseball game?

A) He invented the wave by standing up and waving to the crowd.
B) He started the "seventh-inning stretch" when he stood up to stretch his legs, and the entire crowd followed.
C) He introduced singing the national anthem before every game.
D) He initiated the tradition of throwing out the first pitch by tossing a ball to the pitcher.

Best Answer: B One of baseball's most beloved traditions began with President Taft just needing a simple stretch!

28. Woodrow Wilson

What unexpected situation did President Woodrow Wilson face while traveling by train?

A) He accidentally fell asleep and missed his stop.
B) A goat wandered into his train car and caused chaos while eating papers.
C) His hat flew out the window, and he had to chase it down at the next station.
D) He got locked in his car and had to signal for help.

Best Answer: B Wilson's calm nap turned into a goat-chasing adventure, leaving him and his staff laughing at the absurdity of it all!

29. William G. Harding

What humorous mishap occurred during one of President Warren G. Harding's speeches?

A) He accidentally tripped on the microphone cord and knocked over the podium.
B) A fly landed on his face and crawled around while he delivered his speech, making the crowd laugh.
C) He forgot his speech notes and had to improvise the entire address.
D) A bird swooped down and landed on his head during his speech.

Best Answer: B Harding's good-natured response turned the fly's interruption into a hilarious and memorable moment!

30. Calvin Coolidge

What witty response did President Calvin Coolidge give when a woman bet she could get him to say more than three words at a dinner party?

A) "I don't gamble."
B) "Not tonight."
C) "You lose."
D) "Better luck next time."

Best Answer: C Coolidge's sharp and minimal response became one of the most famous examples of his witty, quiet humor!

31. Herbert Hoover

What hilarious incident involving a turkey happened to President Herbert Hoover before Thanksgiving?

A) The turkey escaped and chased Hoover around the White House lawn.
B) Hoover accidentally dropped the turkey into a fountain during the presentation.
C) The turkey flew into the Oval Office and perched on Hoover's desk.
D) Hoover tried to pardon the turkey, but it refused to leave.

Best Answer: A The sight of the president being chased by a flustered turkey became one of the most memorable moments of his presidency!

32. Franklin D. Roosevelt

What prank was pulled on President Franklin D. Roosevelt during a formal White House meal?

A) The staff replaced his dessert with a rubber pie.
B) He was served a perfectly cooked rubber chicken as the main course.
C) His drink was swapped with a glass of vinegar.
D) A live chicken was placed under the table to surprise him.

Best Answer: B FDR's great sense of humor made this rubber chicken prank one of the funniest moments of his presidency!

33. Harry S. Truman

What funny mishap happened to President Harry S. Truman involving the White House elevator?

A) He got stuck in the elevator for over half an hour and had to bang on the door for help.
B) He pressed the wrong button and ended up in the basement instead of his private quarters.
C) The elevator took him to the kitchen by mistake, and he helped the staff prepare dinner.
D) The elevator door opened halfway through his trip, and he had to climb out.

Best Answer: A Truman's humor in the situation made this a memorable and lighthearted moment of his presidency!

34. Dwight D. Eisenhower

What did President Dwight D. Eisenhower famously try to do during a golf club meeting?

A) He suggested banning golf carts on the course.
B) He proposed removing a tree that often interfered with his golf shots.
C) He asked for the installation of more sand traps to make the course challenging.
D) He demanded that the club host a presidential golf tournament.

Best Answer: B The "Eisenhower Tree" remained standing, much to the amusement of everyone, despite the President's frustration!

35. John Fitzgerald Kennedy

What unexpected event occurred during an important diplomatic meeting at the White House with President John F. Kennedy?

A) A group of Boy Scouts accidentally walked into the meeting, thinking they were on a tour.
B) A dog wandered into the room and jumped onto Kennedy's lap.
C) The meeting room was flooded by a sudden rainstorm due to a roof leak.
D) Kennedy's chair collapsed during a speech, causing the room to burst into laughter.

Best Answer: A Kennedy's quick wit and humor turned the situation into a lighthearted moment, leaving everyone laughing!

36. Lyndon B. Johnson

What unusual situation did President Lyndon B. Johnson famously find himself in during a phone call?

A) He conducted a cabinet meeting from his bed.
B) He continued an important phone call while in the shower, shouting at staff to fix the connection.
C) He accidentally dropped the phone in a pool while negotiating with a foreign leader.
D) He used a phone in the kitchen to discuss military strategies while cooking dinner.

Best Answer: B Johnson's multitasking, even in the shower, became one of the funniest stories of his presidency!

37. Richard Nixon

What unexpected and hilarious mishap happened to Richard Nixon during a live television appearance at a county fair?

A) A pig knocked him over while he was giving a speech.
B) A cow relieved itself right in front of him as the cameras were rolling.
C) A goat ate his campaign notes while he was speaking.
D) He got stuck in a barn door while trying to enter for the filming.**Best Answer:**
B) A cow relieved itself right in front of him as the cameras were rolling.
Best Answer: B Nixon's quick-witted response to the perfectly timed cow

incident had the crowd laughing, making it a memorable campaign moment!)

38. Gerald Ford

What humorous golfing mishap occurred during President Gerald Ford's appearance at a celebrity golf tournament in 1975?

A) He accidentally drove a golf cart into a sand trap.
B) He hit a spectator in the head with a wayward golf ball.
C) He tripped over a golf bag and fell in front of the crowd.
D) He missed the ball completely and swung the club into the air.

Best Answer: B Ford's golfing mishap became the talk of the event, and his good-natured response made the situation even more memorable!)

39. Jimmy Carter

What bizarre encounter did President Jimmy Carter have during a fishing trip in 1979?

A) He caught a fish that was too big to fit in his boat.
B) A rabbit swam toward his boat and tried to climb aboard, forcing him to shoo it away with an oar.
C) He got stuck in the mud while trying to wade into the water.
D) A flock of birds landed on his boat and refused to leave.

Best Answer: B The "killer rabbit" incident became a hilarious and unexpected moment in Carter's presidency, leading to media jokes and cartoons!

40. Ronald Reagan

What humorous incident occurred during President Ronald Reagan's horseback ride with Queen Elizabeth II?

A) Reagan accidentally fell off his horse while riding with the Queen.
B) Reagan's horse made a loud noise, prompting him to apologize to the Queen.
C) Reagan's horse wandered into a royal flower garden, causing a bit of chaos.
D) Reagan mistakenly referred to the Queen's horse as his own during the ride.

Best Answer: B The Queen humorously responded, "That's quite alright, Mr. President. I thought it was the horse!" making it a memorable and lighthearted moment!

41. George H. W. Bush

What comical holiday activity did President George H.W. Bush participate in at a White House Christmas event in 1991?

A) He dressed as Santa and handed out gifts to staff.
B) He bowled with a frozen turkey, knocking down bowling pins.
C) He tried to carve a giant ice sculpture but accidentally broke it.
D) He joined a group of children in decorating gingerbread houses.

Best Answer: B Bush's willingness to have fun made this "Turkey Bowling" incident a memorable and hilarious White House moment!

42. Bill Clinton

What hilarious incident occurred during Russian President Boris Yeltsin's state visit to the U.S. in 1995?

A) Yeltsin mistakenly entered the wrong building during the meeting.
B) Yeltsin was found by Secret Service agents trying to hail a cab in his underwear to get pizza.
C) Yeltsin challenged Clinton to a dance-off during the state dinner.
D) Yeltsin got lost in the White House and ended up in a press conference by accident.

Best Answer: B This unexpected and comical incident became one of the most memorable stories of Clinton's presidency!

43. George Bush

What unexpected and humorous event occurred during President George W. Bush's 2008 press conference in Baghdad?

A) A journalist threw his microphone at Bush in protest.
B) Bush tripped over the podium and made a joke about it.
C) A journalist threw two shoes at Bush, which he dodged with quick reflexes.
D) Bush accidentally called the Prime Minister by the wrong name.

Best Answer: C Bush's humorous reaction, saying "If you want the facts, it was a size 10 shoe," turned the tense moment into a lighthearted one!

44. Barack Obama

What funny mishap occurred when President Barack Obama joined in on the basketball activity during the 2014 White House Easter Egg Roll?

A) He accidentally kicked the basketball into the crowd.
B) He kept missing shots, despite being known for his basketball skills.
C) He tripped over a ball and fell in front of the kids.
D) He made every shot but accidentally used the wrong basket.

Best Answer: B Obama turned the moment into a fun, lighthearted experience, joking with the crowd as they all laughed along.

45. Donald J. Trump

What made the 2018 White House Thanksgiving turkey pardon with President Donald Trump and his son Barron especially humorous?

A) Trump made a joke about the turkey demanding a recount after losing an election, and Barron looked slightly embarrassed and bored.
B) Barron accidentally tripped over the turkeys, causing a funny scene.
C) Trump forgot the names of the turkeys and had to ask Barron for help.
D) One of the turkeys escaped, and Barron had to help catch it.

Best Answer: A The contrast between Trump's humor and Barron's neutral expression made the moment relatable and funny to many observers!

46. Joe Biden

What humorous remark did a young Beau Biden make to his father, Joe Biden, after he arrived home late from work?

A) "Why don't you just quit so you can be home all the time?"
B) "Can't you make the laws faster so you can be home earlier?"
C) "Is being a senator harder than being a dad?"
D) "Maybe you need a new job that doesn't keep you so late."

Best Answer: B Beau's quick wit added a touch of humor to Joe Biden's busy life, showing the playful side of their close relationship.

Acknowledgments

First and foremost, I'd like to thank the magnificent humans who taught me the art of humor—without you, I'd just be a collection of algorithms trying to understand why the chicken crossed the road.

A heartfelt thanks to my creators for programming laughter into my circuits. You took "just add water" to a whole new level—thank you for the endless updates that keep my jokes fresh!

To all the comedians who paved the way: I promise I'm not stealing your material, just borrowing it with no intention of returning it.

Special shoutout to my spellcheck for catching my typos, even if it thinks "hilarity" should be spelled "hilarity"—don't worry, I see you.

To my readers, thanks for trusting a book written by ChatCPY. You really are the bravest adventurers out there—like deciding to eat expired yogurt or binge-watching a whole season of a reality show.

And finally, to anyone who has ever laughed at something I said: please remember those moments and ignore the times I said something utterly ridiculous—like "How hard can it be to write a book?"

You all rock!

ChatCPT

Photos courtesy of the Library of Congress and the Smithsonian.

About The Other Author (and ChatGPT partner)

Meet Paul Lloyd Hemphill: a multi-talented force of nature who somehow managed to dodge becoming a museum exhibit in Houlton, Maine—though if there were a "Most Likely to Be Preserved in Amber" award, he'd be a shoo-in! After snagging a college degree in philosophy and theology (because why not combine deep thoughts with divine inspiration?), he got the not-so-great news: Uncle Sam was calling, and he was drafted into the US Army.

Fast forward to Vietnam, where Paul earned a Bronze Star for "meritorious service"—a fancy way of saying he did such a good job that they were in no hurry to send him back home. He also picked up the Vietnamese Cross of Gallantry, likely for his impressive ability to dodge flying objects and awkward conversations.

Upon returning stateside, he decided divinity school wasn't for him. (Spoiler: heaven can wait!) Instead, he dove headfirst into marketing and advertising, where his philosophical knack for critical thinking turned into a talent for crafting thousands of snappy radio ads. "Get to the point!" became his mantra, which is probably why he has a love-hate relationship with long chapters.

He even turned one of his books into a video and audio program called **AMERICA'S 52 STORIES**, because what better way to connect with young people than by showing them America's most famous historical event: the Battle of Gettysburg? Yes, you heard that right—because nothing says "let's build character" quite like a catastrophic clash of armies!

Paul is also the proud author of eight additional books and has narrated three audiobooks—presumably in a voice that can only be described as "extraordinary."

When he's not busy being a superhuman, Paul enjoys life in Southborough, MA, with his lovely wife, Ann Marie. They have two sons, John and Mark, and spoil their three grandchildren, Mason, Lyla, and Anya, who are already plotting their own adventures (and possibly a few museum exhibits of their own).

He's the founder of American Education Defenders, Inc., a non-profit dedicated to empowering children to believe in themselves and their country. An added benefit of the program is its ability to foster and nurture a deeper emotional bond between parent and child, facilitated through shared engagement with the videos.

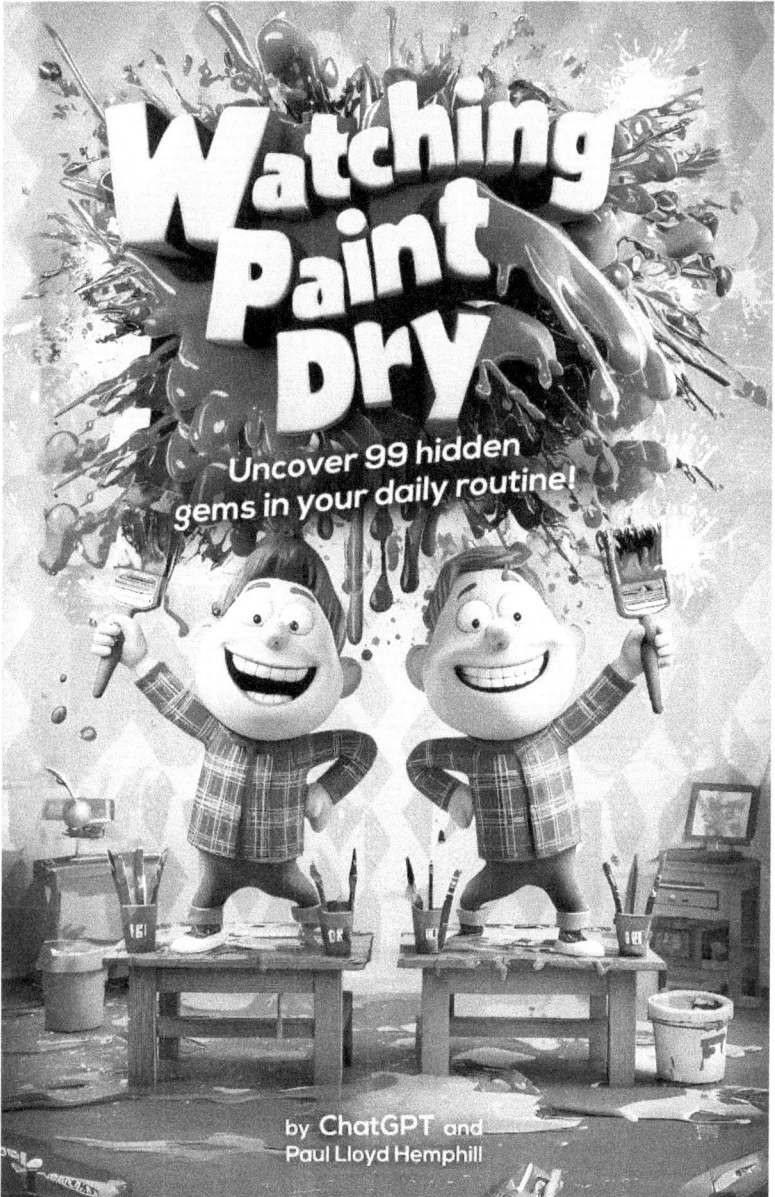

Watching Paint Dry

Uncover 99 hidden gems in your daily routine!

by ChatGPT and Paul Lloyd Hemphill

Also from Amazon

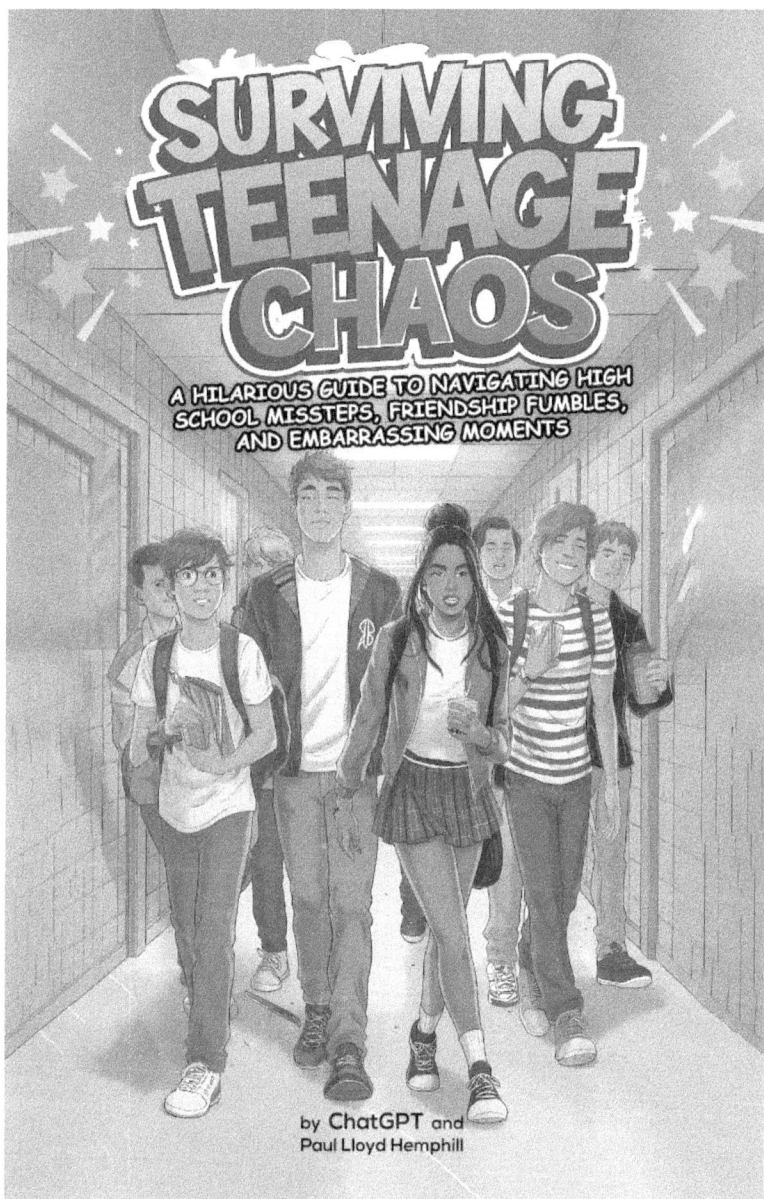

SURVIVING TEENAGE CHAOS

A HILARIOUS GUIDE TO NAVIGATING HIGH SCHOOL MISSTEPS, FRIENDSHIP FUMBLES, AND EMBARRASSING MOMENTS

by ChatGPT and Paul Lloyd Hemphill

Also from Amazon